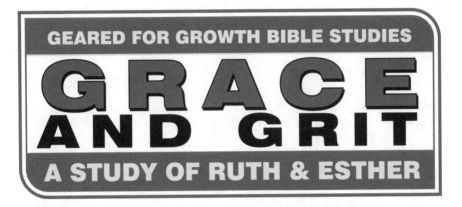

GEARED FOR GROWTH BIBLE STUDIES
GRACE AND GRIT
A STUDY OF RUTH & ESTHER

BIBLE STUDIES TO IMPACT THE LIVES OF ORDINARY PEOPLE

Written by Nina Drew

The Word Worldwide

CHRISTIAN
FOCUS

CONTENTS

QUESTIONS AND NOTES

ANSWER GUIDE

PREFACE

GEARED FOR GROWTH

> 'Where there's LIFE there's GROWTH:
> Where there's GROWTH there's LIFE.'

WHY GROW a study group?

Because as we study the Bible and share together we can

- learn to combat loneliness, depression, staleness, frustration, and other problems
- get to understand and love each other
- become responsive to the Holy Spirit's dealing and obedient to God's Word

and that's GROWTH.

How do you GROW a study group?

- Just start by asking a friend to join you and then aim at expanding your group.
- Study the set portions daily (they are brief and easy: no catches).
- Meet once a week to discuss what you find.
- Befriend others, both Christians and non Christians, and work away together

see how it GROWS!

WHEN you GROW ...

This will happen at school, at home, at work, at play, in your youth group, your student fellowship, women's meetings, mid-week meetings, churches and communities,

you'll be REACHING THROUGH TEACHING

INTRODUCTORY STUDY

Has the thought ever come to you, 'I'd love to ask Paul what he meant by that'? or 'I wonder how Elizabeth really felt when she found herself pregnant at her age!'? Well, we'll have all eternity to talk over such things – if we're still interested! Let's imagine a conversation between Ruth and Esther when they meet.

Esther: It's you, Ruth. I've wanted to meet you. I've always felt a kind of kinship with you. I guess it's partly because we're the only two women to have a book of the Bible called after our names. That was a real honour.

Ruth: Yes, Esther, it was indeed an honour. Yet there must be thousands of unwritten stories of women who have served God more faithfully than we.

Esther: I'm sure of that. One thing I'd like to know Ruth. How did you really feel when you turned your back on your people and country?

Ruth: Oh, Esther ... such mixed feelings. I loved my parents. Yet, after living with Naomi and family, and seeing something of their faith, even though they were not really living in victory, I just couldn't go back to all that idolatry. And, you know, I really loved Naomi. How could I leave that lonely woman to go back and face life alone? Something in me, that I'm sure was the voice of God, was just urging me to go on with her. And, of course, I came to see more and more that God was showering on me blessings and favours I didn't deserve.

Esther: And time proved your decision to be right! A wonderful husband and family, and the honour of being one through whom our Saviour was born.

Ruth: But tell me something about yourself. How did you feel when you were taken off to the palace to be one of the candidates for becoming Queen?

Esther: Scared stiff. And, oh, so insecure. I kept thinking of those times when Mordecai used to tell me stories of God's dealings with our nation, and when we prayed together, I knew he was praying for me in that ungodly atmosphere. You know, Ruth, I felt right from the start that God had some hidden purpose in it all. I would never have had the courage apart from that prayer-backing and the knowledge of God with me.

Ruth: God's ways are wonderful. You know, in looking back I see God was ordering every detail of our lives, although we didn't always understand it at the time.

Esther: Yes, even to you, a Gentile marrying a Jew, and me a Jewess marrying a Gentile!

Ruth: And now we can see the time down there as a sort of probationary period to prepare us for this tremendous life. Why, even the love I felt for Boaz seems a dim reflection of the real thing, the love my heart feels towards Jesus! I know I wasn't always as faithful as I should have been. But Esther, He's forgiven all our mistakes – His grace is so wonderful. We know we haven't only been cleansed from all our sins, but have been completely transformed! And we will live for ever and ever in this tremendous fullness of life.

Esther: Yes, and now we know God in a very real way as Father, and we're part of His wonderful family. All the redeemed ones throughout all the ages are now our brothers and sisters, and we'll always be together. No more partings or sorrows and problems. How could we have dreamed in those days that this bliss would be ours, Ruth?

As we commence this study on the life of Ruth and Esther, two adjectives pop right into my mind. Regarding Ruth, we see the marvellous GRACE of God which lifts the sinner out of 'lostness' and into the glorious family of God.

On the other hand, Esther, already numbered amongst God's children, manifests real FORTITUDE in a situation beyond human hope. Our study has been entitled, 'GRACE AND GRIT', therefore, before we go on to study these two women and God's design working out in their lives, let's have a look at some of the Biblical concepts of these terms.

GRACE: In Greek this word is CHARIS and in its context here means 'the spontaneous mercy of God which brings pleasure, delight and beauty to the recipient.' (W. E. Vine) Webster's Dictionary defines it, 'the undeserved mercy of God'.

Look up the following references to get a glimpse of Grace – God's gift operating in and through the life of the believer.

Romans 5:2; 1 Peter 5:12; 2 Peter 3:18; 2 Corinthians 8:6, 9; 9:8; Romans 1:5; 12:6; 15:15; 1 Corinthians 3:10; Galatians 2:9.

GRIT: The Greek word for courage or boldness is THARREO. It carries with it the thought of warmth (indicating confidence in contrast with the chill of fear). Webster gives, 'firmness of character or spirit' as the meaning of grit; for courage, 'the quality that enables men to meet danger without fear', for bold, 'courageous or performed with spirit'.

Look up the following references and be encouraged that 'God has not given us the spirit of fear, but of ability to achieve...' (2 Tim. 1:7). Where did these people get their courage?

Mark 15:43; John 11:16; Acts 3:12-26; 5:21; 29-32; 20:22-24.

Look up also:

Proverbs 28:1; 1 Corinthians 16:13; 2 Corinthians 5:6, 8; 10:1; 11:21; Ephesians 3:12; Philippians 1:14; Hebrews 4:16; 10:19; 13:6; 1 John 2:28; 4:17.

As we go on with this study, pray for one another that you will experience more of God's grace and courage in your daily living.

STUDY 1

COMPROMISE AND RESTORATION
– A STUDY ON CHOICES

QUESTIONS

DAY 1 *Ruth 1:1, 2; Psalm 46:1.*
a) Why did Elimelech and his family move to Moab?

b) Have you ever moved house? Did you have any problems? When problems confront us where is the place of safety?

DAY 2 *Ruth 1:3-5; 2 Corinthians 6:14.*
Naomi must have arranged her sons' marriages to non-Jewish girls with their consent. Discuss the subject of mixed marriages.

DAY 3 *Ruth 1:6-10; Isaiah 30:15.*
a) What induced Naomi to return to her own country?

b) The two non-Israelite girls had been kind to their husbands and Naomi. People today are quick to point out that some non-Christians are 'nicer' people than some Christians. How can this be?

DAY 4 *Ruth 1:11-15; Joshua 24:15; Matthew 10:37, 38.*
a) On what grounds was Orpah induced to return to her Moabite relations?

b) Naomi did not encourage the girls to accompany her, but rather emphasized the difficulties. Compare that with Jesus' attitude (Matt. 8:20; 16:24; Luke 14:28).

c) What are the dangers in persuading people to follow Christ by emphasizing only the benefits?

DAY 5 *Ruth 1:16-18; Deuteronomy 30:19, 20.*
a) What induced Ruth to make her decision?

b) What were some of the difficulties in making such a decision and commitment?

DAY 6 *Ruth 1:19, 20; Galatians 6:1; Philemon 1:15, 16.*
a) No word of reproof from the Bethlehemites, only welcome. Apply this to situations in which we may be involved.

b) Why the surprise expressed in 'Can this be Naomi?'?

DAY 7 *Ruth 1:21, 22; Hebrews 12:9-11.*
a) How does Naomi's comment on her name tell us something of her reaction to God's dealings with her?

b) What would have been a more positive attitude for her to take?

NOTES

The Bible tells us that God loves everybody, that Jesus Christ is the Saviour of the whole world. Yet God first chose and prepared one nation as a vehicle to show His glory to the world. Israel was to be a holy nation, kept free from the defilement of the surrounding nations with their idolatry, immorality and sex perversions. One such evil nation was Moab. The father of this nation was born through incest between Lot and his daughter.

This was the nation which hired Balaam to curse Israel, and which led Israel into immorality (Gen. 19:30-37; Num. 22:1–25:3). Yet we shall see in this beautiful story of Ruth that God has His chosen people even in the worst environments.

ELIMELECH'S AND NAOMI'S CHOICE

Now let us come to our story. The story of Ruth was contemporary with Judges (Ruth 1:1). At the time the story opens, Israel was being disciplined by God. Famine had visited the land, and probably attacks were being made by their enemies the Midianites (Judg. 6:1). When God brings disciplines into our lives what do we do?

Admit where we've gone wrong and ask God to forgive us
Try to escape God's disciplines and seek refuge in worldly company?

The latter was the choice of Elimelech, Naomi and their two sons. (See also Gen. 12:10; 26:1-4.) How often the grass looks greener on the other side of the fence! Our life, like Elimelech's, consists of choices or decisions, and the choices we make through life determine where we are spiritually today.

This family chose to leave their home in Bethlehem (ironically it means 'House of Bread'!), to seek refuge in Moab, fifty miles east across the Jordan. They went 'for a while' (v. 1, NIV), but they were soon absorbed into the life of the country, and remained there ten years. Elimelech died. The sons married Moabite women. But before any children were born to them, tragedy again struck. Mahlon and Chilion died, leaving the three women, widows.

RUTH'S AND ORPAH'S CHOICE

Now the test comes. Naomi sees in this tragedy the judgment of God. She makes the right decision to turn to the people of God. Her two daughters-in-law also have to make a big decision:

Remain in Moab with their own people and their Moabite gods or
Emigrate to Israel to a new people and the worship of the living God?

Orpah made the first choice. Ruth the second. This could be termed Ruth's conversion. Her commitment was complete. Have you made Ruth's choice?

For Naomi and Ruth the irrevocable choice has been made – God, and the fellowship of His people. The long journey proceeds, and eventually two very weary women reach Bethlehem, their home. They are welcomed by the townspeople – her real family.

MEMORY VERSE: '... I have set before you life and death, blessings and curses. Now choose life ...' (Deut. 30:19).

STUDY 2

LOVE BLOSSOMING

QUESTIONS

DAY 1   *Ruth 2:1; Isaiah 55:8, 9.*
The writer now gives us a preview of the man Boaz. Why would the description of Boaz make him an unlikely choice for Ruth?

DAY 2   *Ruth 2:2; Leviticus 19:9, 10; Deuteronomy 24:19; Luke 6:1.*
a) Discuss the Jewish customs of allowing the poor and foreigner to glean in fields and vineyards. Are we, in contrast to eastern countries, too possessive of our property?

b) Comment on the attitude of the two women to each other, as seen in Ruth 2:2.

DAY 3   *Ruth 2:3; Genesis 24; 1 Samuel 9; etc. (Try to read these in modern versions.)*
a) Think of other incidents from the Bible or from your own life where things that just seem to 'happen' turn out to have great significance.

b) What is one aspect of guidance that we can learn from this?

DAY 4   *Ruth 2:4; Luke 7:2, 3; Ephesians 6:5-9; 1 Peter 2:17a.*
a) What could be learned by employers and employees in the attitudes shown in these verses?

b) In what other relationships in life should the same principles work out?

c) What is meant by the word 'bless'? Whom should we bless? (Ps. 103:I; 129:8; Matt. 5:44)

DAY 5 *Ruth 2:5-16; Matthew 5:41.*
a) As seen in these verses, describe the qualities of (1) Boaz (2) Ruth.

b) Can Jesus' principle of 'going the second mile' be seen in Boaz? How can we apply this to our lives?

DAY 6 *Ruth 2:17-19.*
a) What might Naomi's thoughts have been while Ruth was away?

b) What did Ruth bring home that made Naomi exclaim with pleasure?

DAY 7 *Ruth 2:20-23; 2 Thessalonians 3:10; James 2:17.*
We now see a remarkable change from Naomi's attitude of self-pity and hopelessness (Ruth 1:20, 21) to joy and thankfulness. How can God use us to bring about a like change in other embittered people?

NOTES

God honours Ruth's choice to identify with God and His people. Now we see His beautiful purposes for this young woman beginning to take shape – purposes which she never could have imagined the day she chose to turn her back on her past life. So many things in a Christian's life which seem like coincidences are really the unseen overruling hand of God at work. So often these things happen naturally as we go about our usual tasks. So with Ruth. We notice that Ruth is not one to sit down idly and wait for food to fall into her lap. Neither did she want to see her dear mother-in-law take on the backbreaking and humiliating task of gleaning grain in the harvest fields. (Background reading: Matt. 6:25-34; I Cor. 13.)

GOD'S PLAN UNFOLDING
God directed her steps to the area owned by the wealthy Boaz. She did not presume to start work without obtaining permission (Ruth 2:7), and soon a heavy day's work was underway.
Of all the young women gleaning barley that day, God caused Boaz's eyes to alight on Ruth, and he enquired about her. Yes, and was it God who caused his interest in her to develop into something more substantial? He admired her greatly for her deep devotion to the widowed Naomi, and that admiration began to blossom into love. He also recognized in Ruth a young woman with a deep faith in the living God 'under whose wings you have come to take refuge' (Ps. 63:7; Matt. 23:37).

BOAZ'S ATTITUDE TO RUTH
Probably marriage was far from Boaz's thoughts at that time. After all Ruth was much younger than he (Ruth 3:10), and from a very different background. But the growing love he felt for her was clearly shown in practical ways. After all, love is not just FEELING but DOING. Otherwise, how could God COMMAND us to love Him, each other and our enemies?

LOVE SEEN IN ACTION. Let us see how Boaz's love was expressed:

Ruth 2:8 – By giving protection.
Ruth 2:9 – By giving water that was already drawn.
Ruth 2:14 – By giving food prepared for the servants.
Ruth 2:16 – By giving provision for the future.

RUTH'S ATTITUDE TO BOAZ
Ruth's attitude to Boaz was, as is proper, one of respect and humility, yet warmth and gratitude. If her heart missed a beat or two, she would hardly harbour any thoughts of marriage with a man of such wealth and importance. But we know that 'He gives the very best to those who leave the choice to Him', and this would be the attitude of these two godly people. It applies to marriage, but also to many other aspects of our lives.

MEMORY VERSE: 'Dear friends, let us love one another, for love comes from God. Everyone who loves has been born of God and knows God' (I John 4:7, NIV).

STUDY 3

BOAZ, THE KINSMAN-REDEEMER

QUESTIONS

DAY 1 *Ruth 3:1.*
Naomi wants to seek security for Ruth. What are some of the beautiful metaphors in the Bible that tell us where our spiritual security lies? Think some out before looking up: Psalm 23:1; 91:1; 18:2; Proverbs 18:10; etc.

DAY 2 *Ruth 3:2, 3.*
Ruth was told to (a) wash herself, (b) anoint herself (with perfumed oil), (c) put on her best clothes. She was to meet her future bridegroom. Can you find some spiritual significance in this preparation?
(Try: (a) Titus 3:5; Ephesians 5:26;

(b) Isaiah 61:1; Acts 10:38;

(c) Isaiah 61:3, 10; Revelation 19:8)

DAY 3 *Ruth 3:4-7; Exodus 19:5; 1 Peter 3:1; Ephesians 6:1, 5; 1 Peter 5:5; Philippians 2:8, 9.*
a) Ruth obeyed Naomi implicitly because she loved and trusted her. To whom should we submit ourselves?

b) Can you quote one supreme example of where obedience led to joy and victory?

DAY 4 *Ruth 3:8, 9; I Timothy 5:8; Matthew 15:4-7.*
a) Ruth's request was on the basis of relationship. Duty towards relations is clearly expressed in the Bible. Comment on ways people in the West today avoid this.

b) What practical steps could we take to improve family relationships?

DAY 5 *Ruth 3:10, 11; Proverbs 31:10-12.*
a) How did the prospect of Boaz marrying a Gentile woman differ from the cases discussed in Ruth I?

b) Discuss together some other admirable women in the Bible.

DAY 6 *Ruth 3:12-15; 2 Corinthians 8:21; Colossians 3:12; Hebrews 13:18.*
a) Boaz wanted to marry Ruth, yet would not go over the head of the relative with prior claim. What does this tell us of Boaz?

b) How does he show his concern for Ruth's good name?

DAY 7 *Ruth 3:16-18; Psalm 37:9; 40:1; Isaiah 40:31.*
a) A day of patient waiting! Describe Naomi's and Ruth's thoughts during this time.

b) Naomi was confident that Boaz wouldn't let the grass grow under his feet. What does this say for the man?

NOTES

THE JEWISH CUSTOM OF KINSMAN-REDEEMER

To understand the passage before us, we must take a look at the Jewish custom concerning inheritance. Elimelech had owned a piece of land that had apparently been worked by his relatives after his emigration to Moab. Legally, this land would have been passed on to his sons Mahlon and Chilion, and to their sons. But Mahlon and Chilion had died without children. The custom in such a case was for the deceased's brother or nearest kinsman to marry the widow, to raise up children to inherit the deceased brother's property. The first son so born would be considered, not the son of the natural father, but of the deceased relative. The kinsman who married the young widow would be known as a 'Goel' meaning Kinsman-Redeemer. (Background Reading: Deut. 25:5, 6.)

THE PLAN

Naomi desired two things for her family:

1. That the name of her husband should not be cut off from Israel through their having no descendants.
2. That her lovely young daughter-in-law should have the joy and security of marriage and children.

Did Naomi know of the existence of the nearer kinsman than Boaz? Perhaps so. But Boaz was her choice for Ruth. Although Boaz and Ruth would have seen a good deal of each other during the 3 or 4 months till the end of the wheat harvest, they would have had no opportunity for private talk. The subject of Boaz taking on the duty of kinsman redeemer must be discussed with him, but away from prying eyes and ears. Ruth would be totally dependent on her mother-in-law for guidance in so delicate a matter. Naomi hit on a plan.

We hold our breath as we peep into the intimate details of this chapter. Can't you hear Naomi praying as Ruth sets out on her mission: 'Oh God, don't let anyone see her or overhear their conversation. Let Boaz desire her greatly. It's in Your hands Lord.'

THE OUTCOME

God certainly had everything in hand. It all went according to plan. Maybe Boaz woke up in the night with cold feet to the alluring perfume that betrayed the presence of the lovely girl. Was Boaz a lonely widower? Or a bachelor? The Book is silent on this point. We know that his heart leaped to Ruth's proposal. He was not doing her a favour, but she was doing him a wonderful kindness. He spread his covering around her shoulders as a sign of his taking on her protection in marriage (Ezek. 16:8b). Early dawn saw the two women rejoicing together at the prospect of Ruth's engagement to Boaz being finalized that day.

'Cover me, cover me. Extend the border of Thy mantle over me,
Because Thou art my nearest Kinsman. Cover me, cover me, cover me.'

MEMORY VERSE: 'All the ways of the LORD are loving and faithful for those who keep the demands of his covenant' (Ps. 25:10, NIV).

STUDY 4

QUESTIONS

DAY 1   *Ruth 4:1-4.*
a) 'The gate' was the law court of that day, and Boaz was obviously a man of importance. What was the legal matter to be decided?

b) Was the 'nearer kinsman' prepared to redeem Elimelech's land?

DAY 2   *Ruth 4:5, 6.*
a) Why do you think the next of kin was unwilling to marry Ruth?

b) What would Boaz's reaction have been to his decision?

DAY 3   *Ruth 4:7-10; Deuteronomy 25:5-10; Job 19:25; Galatians 3:13, 14.*
a) How had the custom outlined in Deuteronomy 25 been modified in Ruth's case?

b) Boaz has redeemed Ruth from poverty and loneliness to become his bride. Was this redemption voluntary or obligatory? Apply this to our Kinsman-Redeemer.

DAY 4   *Ruth 4:11, 12; Galatians 5:22-23.*
a) The prayer of the elders was that Ruth should be fruitful. What are some of the fruit that God looks for in our lives?

b) 'May you be renowned in Bethlehem,' was prophetic. How was it fulfilled?

DAY 5 *Ruth 4:13; Ephesians 5:25-33; Hosea 2:19, 20; 2 Corinthians 11:2; Revelation 19:7, 8.*
a) What is the teaching in Ephesians 5 regarding relationships of husband and wife?

b) Spiritualized, what then is the relationship of Christ and His bride, the Church? When will the fullness of this relationship be experienced?

DAY 6 *Ruth 4:14-17; 2 Timothy 1:5.*
a) The people recognized the birth of the child as a precious gift from God, both to parents and grandmother. Comment on this.

b) What can we learn from the relationship between Naomi and Ruth here?

DAY 7 *Ruth 4:18-22; Romans 5:20; 2 Corinthians 6:14.*
a) Mahlon had disobeyed God in marrying a Gentile unbeliever. But now we see that God's grace is bigger even than our mistakes. Can you think of any other instances of this?

b) Can this gracious intervention of God justify believers in marrying nonbelievers? Why?

c) Share with the group which aspect of this lovely story has been the greatest blessing to you.

NOTES

We can all breathe again! Ruth and Boaz are married. A son, Obed, (meaning 'servant of the Lord') is born, not only to the happy couple, but to Naomi. 'A son has been born to Naomi', a son to carry on the family name and the family inheritance. And now the story of Ruth is complete. Ruth, a Gentile (non-Jew), a former idol-worshipper, by his grace has come under the shadow of the wings of the living God of Israel. She is married to a splendid man, and has become an ancestor, not only of Kind David, but of our Lord Jesus Christ Himself. What an honour!

> Amazing grace, how sweet the sound that saved a wretch like me,
> I once was lost, but now I'm found, was blind, but now I see.

THE SPIRITUAL MEANING OF THE BOOK OF RUTH
This is an historical record. Yet, as with so many other books of the Old Testament, a wonderful spiritual meaning emerges, that can be a great blessing to us. Let us look at the spiritual meaning of these two lovers.

BOAZ is a type of Jesus Christ, our Kinsman-Redeemer. Our Kinsman, because He left heaven, and took on Himself our human nature and became one of us. Our Redeemer, because He loved us dearly, loved us enough to give His life to buy us for Himself. Like Boaz, He was rich. He has a Name above every name, is Owner of the universe. Yet He loves you and me, and paid the ransom to make us His own.

RUTH is a type of the Church consisting of all those who have been redeemed by Jesus and who have become His own. We, too, are not of the nation of Israel, but are Gentiles, outsiders. But Jesus loved us, chose us, redeemed us, and called us 'beloved', His bride. (Meditate on the 'Song of Solomon'.) This can only take place when we said 'yes' to Him. Have you said 'yes'?

Boaz and Ruth became fruitful parents. And, in union with Christ, we too can become fruitful Christians. We can only bear fruit in union with Him. 'That you might be joined to another, to Him that was raised from the dead, that we might bear fruit for God' (Rom. 7:4).

Whatever difficulties come your way, remember, your heavenly Boaz is by your side, loving you, encouraging you. Sink into His loving arms. Look to Him always, as we may be sure Ruth did to the husband she adored. Our welfare and happiness are His concern. Let us be sure that we make His happiness our chief concern.

MEMORY VERSE: For your Maker is your husband – the LORD Almighty is his name – the Holy One of Israel is your Redeemer' (Isa. 54:5, NIV).

INTRODUCTORY STUDY

ESTHER

HISTORICAL BACKGROUND

This very dramatic story of Esther is set in the land of Persia (now Iran) during the fifth century BC, about six centuries after the book of RUTH. The Jewish nation had backslidden from God, and had gone into idolatry and many other forms of evil. They had refused to listen to the warnings of godly prophets such as Jeremiah, and consequently God had allowed them to be taken captive into Babylon. Later the nations of Media and Persia had overrun Babylon, and extended their empire from India to Ethiopia in the south, and west to the Mediterranean Sea.

The first king of Persia, Cyrus, offered the Jews freedom to return to Jerusalem and permission to rebuild the temple of God, but only 42,360 people (Ezra 2:64) elected to go. The remainder, having by now well integrated into the Persian system, were content to remain in the land. Cyrus was followed by Darius, and Darius by Ahasuerus (also known by his Greek name of Xerxes). It was during his reign that the events of ESTHER took place. A playwright would find difficulty in creating a plot producing such suspense and excitement as we find in this little book.

It is surprising that the name of God is not mentioned in the book, except in acrostic form, which can be seen in the Hebrew, but not in the English. The unknown author was obviously a Jew. But was he a historian, who was more interested in relating the historical facts than revealing its spiritual message? We do not know. But we do know that no book in the Bible shows more clearly the overruling, protecting hand of God than this little gem.

Romans 15:4 tells us, 'For everything that was written in the past was written to teach us, so that through endurance and the encouragement of the Scriptures we might have hope' (NIV).

Let us see what encouragement this little book can bring to us.

STUDY 5

AHASUERUS' FEAST –
QUEEN VASHTI REPLACED BY ESTHER

QUESTIONS

DAY 1   *Esther 1:1-9; Daniel 5:28-30; 6:1-6.*
What does the six months' feast tell us of the Persian kingdom and its king?

DAY 2   *Esther 1:10-12; Proverbs 18:22; 19:14; Colossians 3:18.*
a) What was the king's motive in commanding Vashti to be brought to his feast?

b) Discuss Vashti's disobedience, and the subject of submission of wives to their husbands.

DAY 3   *Esther 1:13-22; Proverbs 5:18, 19; Isaiah 54:6-8; 1 Peter 3:7.*
a) What was the advice of the seven-man cabinet to the king?

b) Were there any grounds for the fears they expressed?

DAY 4   *Esther 2:1-4; 1 Corinthians 7:2, 4; 13:4-7; Ephesians 5:21-33; 4:32.*
a) On what qualifications was the king to choose his queen?

b) What are the main requirements you feel necessary for a happy marriage?

DAY 5 *Esther 2:5-7.*
a) What do these verses tell us of Mordecai?
Deuteronomy 12:28, 29; Psalm 41:1; 68:5; James 1:27; 1 Peter 3:4.

b) Comment on the description of Esther as *'beautiful and lovely'*, and relate this to ourselves as Christians, (See also verse Esther 2:15b.)

DAY 6 *Esther 2:8-11; Genesis 39:1-4, 19-22; 2 Kings 5:2, 3; Acts 16:24, 25.*
Esther found herself in a situation she would never have chosen. If we find ourselves in undesirable circumstances, what should be our attitude?

DAY 7 *Esther 2:12-18; Romans 8:28; 1 Corinthians 9:24, 25; Philippians 4:11-13.*
a) Try to put yourself in Esther's situation. What would be her feelings as winner of the 'beauty contest'?

b) And the feelings of the many losers, condemned to be mere chattels kept in the king's harem for his possible pleasure? Comment on the position of women today in comparison with this period of history.

NOTES

THE STATUS OF WOMEN

Persia (Iran) along with many other Muslim countries, is governed by strict Islamic rules which includes a suppression of its women.

As we look back over twenty-one centuries to the same area before Christ and before Mohammed, we find that the status of women is little better than it is there today. Only in Christ is there full emancipation and fulfilment.

THE EASTERN KING

The book opens with a magnificent show of pomp and wealth by a proud, ambitious and self-seeking king. After showing off all his wealth to his admiring guests, the king looks around for something further to impress them. Ah, yes, his beautiful Queen! The chamberlains hurry off to bring her at the king's command, but Queen Vashti refuses to come. Imagine the king's chagrin. His dignity has been publicly affronted!

QUEEN VASHTI'S DISOBEDIENCE

Why did Vashti refuse to come to the king? Was it an early expression of 'Women's Lib' spirit? ('Why should I leave my guests to obey his whims?') Or did she shrink from appearing before the king and his drinking party, unveiled? This was against Persian custom. Whatever her reason, this one act of disobedience cost her her crown.

VASHTI'S REPLACEMENT BY ESTHER

A lustful king was not short of women. He had many beauties in his harem. But one outstanding one must be found to replace Vashti as queen, and to keep the dynasty alive by producing a royal son. Esther, as an orthodox Jewess, would hardly have sought after this 'honour', but God, who knows the end from the beginning, overruled in the choice.

Later her guardian and cousin, the noble Mordecai, was to say, 'Who knows whether you have come to the kingdom for such a time as this?', a time when her race was in danger of extermination.

Do you remember how Joseph had said several centuries earlier, 'You meant it for evil, but God meant it for good, to save many people alive' (Gen. 50:20)?

God is on the throne, and without overriding our free wills, He is yet ruling the affairs of nations, as well as in the circumstances of our individual lives.

MEMORY VERSE: 'In all your ways acknowledge him, and he will make your paths straight (Prov. 3:6, NIV).

ESTHER • STUDY 5 • AHASUERUS' FEAST

STUDY 6

HAMAN'S RISE TO POWER –
CONFLICT OF GOOD AND EVIL

QUESTIONS

DAY 1   *Esther 2:19-23; Nehemiah 1:11; Jeremiah 29:7; Daniel 1:19, 20; I Timothy 2:1, 2; Romans 13:5-7.*
a) Mordecai teaches us a lesson in loyalty to our country and rulers. Give other examples of Jews who faithfully held positions of authority during this period of exile.

b) How can we take an effective part in the affairs of our country?

DAY 2   *Esther 3:1, 2a; Proverbs 8:13; 29:23; Daniel 4:37; I John 2:16.*
a) Success went to Haman's head and caused him to lord it over others. In what realms can this happen today?

b) What are some realms in which WE may be tempted to show pride? And what is the remedy?

DAY 3   *Esther 3:2b, 4; Daniel 3:6; Genesis 39.*
a) Give other examples from the Bible of people who refused to compromise in what they knew to be right.

b) And of others who went against their consciences for personal gain or to please men (e.g. Gen. 12:13; John 19:4, 16; Gal. 2:11, 12; etc.).

DAY 4   *Esther 3:5-7: Matthew 5:10, 11; 25:40.*
a) Who is a modern counterpart of Haman in his hatred of the Jews?

b) If we are in Christ we are the spiritual Israel (Gal. 3:29), and therefore Satan opposes us as he did the Jews. How?

c) What can we do for fellow Christians who are being persecuted for their faith?

DAY 5   *Esther 3:8, 9: Exodus 20:16; John 8:44.*
a) Why do you think the king readily cooperated with Haman's schemes?

b) What can we learn from his mistake?

DAY 6   *Esther 3:10, 11; Luke 9:1; 10:17-19; Matthew 28:19, 20; 2 Peter 1:3.*
The signet ring was a sign of the king's authority. Our King has also given us His authority. For what purpose?
By what means? (Matt. 4:4, 7, 10; Rev. 12:11; Acts 1:8; 4:7-10; Eph. 6:11.)

DAY 7   *Esther 3:12-15; Mark 16:15; Ephesians 6:18, 19; Philippians 4:14-19; Acts 8:4.*
Haman showed great enthusiasm in getting his evil message out to every part of his empire.
What means can we use to get the good news of salvation out to the world? Consider, prayerfully, what you are doing about this.

NOTES

MORDECAI'S LOYALTY (Ch. 2:19-23)

Mordecai must have had some official position as 'sitting in the king's gate' (cf. Ruth 4:1; Gen. 23:10). He was an employee of the palace, probably a gatekeeper. In this position he would have ample opportunity to hear of a plot being hatched by two palace guards against the life of the king. Was it chance or God that caused him to hear about it, that put Esther in a position where she could reach the king with the information, and that later caused the king to read the record of it at the psychological moment? Every minor detail in this book assures us that God is engineering the circumstances of our lives.

RISE OF HAMAN (Ch. 3:1)

'Haman the Agagite' – this description of Haman speaks volumes! The Amalekites had always been the enemies of the Jews. God had commanded, through Moses, that they should remember the Amalekites' enmity and 'blot out their remembrance from under heaven' (Exod. 17:14). Later God commanded King Saul to utterly destroy the Amalekites, but Saul spared Agag, their king. The former kingdom of the Amalekites was now part of the Persian kingdom and Haman, the Agagite, was probably a prince of that kingdom. He rapidly rose to be the king's favourite.

HAMAN'S PLOT AGAINST THE JEWS (Ch. 3:2-15)

Haman was probably expecting not only respect, but worship, from his subjects. Mordecai, an orthodox Jew, refused to bow to any man, especially a proud, unscrupulous Amalekite. And Haman's revenge? 'He disdained to lay hands on Mordecai alone.' Why not destroy the whole race? The king would ratify any plan he made, without question.

Next, we see him in the presence of the king unfolding his well thought-out plot. 'A certain people' dispersed throughout the kingdom, do not keep the king's laws. They must be destroyed. And to make the plan more attractive, a promise of several million pounds is made, presumably to offset the cost of getting the decrees sent out. Did he expect to recover this money from the loot to be taken from the destroyed Jews? The gullible and greedy Ahasuerus falls into the trap. The signet ring changes hands, and Haman gets to work.

Hundreds of scribes from every language area. Thousands of copies of the edict. Couriers on horseback, with fresh horses supplied at each stage. And, eventually, a copy of the edict is displayed in every village square throughout the vast empire. The Jewish nation will soon be exterminated!

And so the conflict starts. Not only a conflict between the Jews and the anti-Semitists, but a conflict between good and evil; between God and Satan. God has already told us what will be the outcome of that conflict that still rages today (1 Cor. 15:25; Heb. 2:14, 15).

MEMORY VERSE: 'Be self-controlled and alert. Your enemy the devil prowls around like a roaring lion looking for someone to devour. Resist him, standing firm in the faith' (1 Pet. 5:8, 9a, NIV).

STUDY 7

ESTHER THE INTERCESSOR

QUESTIONS

DAY 1 *Esther 4:1-3; 1 Samuel 30:4-6; Nehemiah 1:4; Psalm 18:6; John 11:35.*
a) In what ways was the distress of the Jewish people expressed?

b) In times of sorrow should we:
(1) Express hopeless lamentation?

(2) Show the stiff upper lip?

(3) Weep and express sorrow, while praying and putting our trust in God?

(4) ?

DAY 2 *Esther 4:4-7; 2 Samuel 9:1; Matthew 5:43-45; Luke 10:27-37; Galatians 6:10.*
a) Esther, in her protected environment, was unaware of the distress outside. How can we overcome a like situation?

b) Mordecai knew more than the edict revealed – rumour had got around of the exact sum of Haman's bribe. What lesson is there for us in this? (Num. 32:23b; Matt. 12:35-37; Luke 12:3)

DAY 3 *Esther 4:8, 9; 6:13; John 17:9; Colossians 1:9; 2 Thessalonians 1:11.*
a) What did Mordecai charge Esther to do?

b) Note that Mordecai calls the Jews 'her people'. Who are OUR people for whom we are responsible to make intercession?

DAY 4   *Esther 4:10-14; Romans 8:28; 1 Timothy 6:6.*
a) Express the meaning of verse 14 in your own words.

b) What difference will the assurance that we are in our present situation by God's appointment make to our lives.

DAY 5   *Esther 4:15-17; Daniel 2:17-19; Acts 12:12; 13:1-3.*
a) Though Esther alone was to face the king, she needed the support of the whole Jewish community. Are there other examples of this:
(1) In the Bible?

(2) In your experience?

b) Discuss the issue of 'fasting' and whether there is need to do this today.

DAY 6   *Esther 5:1-4; Isaiah 61:3, 10; Zechariah 3:3, 4.*
a) Esther put on her royal robes to approach the king.

b) What royal 'robe' should we be clothed with when we come before our King on behalf of others?

DAY 7   *Esther 5:5-8; Psalm 25:9; 31:15; 32:8; Romans 8:14, 26.*
Why did Esther still postpone the presenting of her request?

NOTES

LAMENTATION AMONG THE JEWS

The copies of the decree are raced throughout the empire, bringing in their wake unrestrained sorrow and despair. Mordecai is aghast as he realizes the extent of Haman's retaliation. Mordecai is well known in the palace, and although no one knew of the relationship between him and Esther, his strange attire is at least a news item to relieve the boredom of the harem. Esther, in deep concern, sends a servant with clothes to replace his sackcloth rags. These are refused. She then sends another servant to ask the cause of his sorrow. No copy of the decree had, of course, been displayed within the harem – it could hardly affect anyone there! Or could it?

Mordecai sends Esther a copy of the decree, and makes it clear to her that she will be under no special protection. The days of self-humbling and prayer have brought this man into a place of deep faith. He knows that if Esther doesn't meet the challenge, God will somehow send deliverance. But he believes God has put her where she is for this very emergency.

ESTHER ACCEPTS THE CHALLENGE

Let us try to understand Esther's hesitation. Remember how the king had fallen madly in love with her the moment he first set eyes on her? But we wonder what sort of love a man like this is capable of knowing. He has not seen her for thirty days! She knows him well enough to be terrified at the very thought of breaking the palace tradition that no one appear before him without being summoned. Haman may do so, but not she, the queen!

She realizes, however, the seriousness of the hour and accepts the challenge. She makes one condition. All the Jews of the city must unite for three days of prayer and fasting. She and her maids will do likewise.

The three days are up. Esther dons her loveliest robes and approaches the king. As he gazes at her, something of that initial love burns again in his heart. He holds out the golden sceptre (sign of her acceptance), and invites her to state her request. God has shown Esther His strategy. She is not to blurt out her complaints, but await His timing.

The banquet had been prepared in advance, evidence of the assurance God had already given her, and it is not long before the king and Haman are her honoured guests. Still she does not feel the time is ripe to make her request, but she promises the king she will make it at tomorrow's banquet.

How curious the king must have been – and Haman!

MEMORY VERSE: 'If my people, who are called by my name, will humble themselves and pray and seek my face and turn from their wicked ways, then will I hear from heaven and will forgive their sin and will heal their land' (2 Chron. 7:14, NIV).

STUDY 8

OVERTHROW OF HAMAN

QUESTIONS

DAY 1 *Esther 5:9-14; Matthew 5:21, 22; Hebrews 12:15; 1 Peter 5:6.*
a) We see here a conflict of joy and hatred in Haman. How can hatred or resentment rob us of joy?

b) Whom else can it affect?

DAY 2 *Esther 6:1-5; Genesis 24:42-46; 1 Samuel 9:3-17; Psalm 31:15a; Galatians 4:4.*
a) What instances of God's amazing timings can we see here?

b) Have you any similar instances to share from your life or from books you have read?

DAY 3 *Esther 6:6-13; Proverbs 16:18; Daniel 4:28-37; Luke 18:9-14.*
Can you visualize the effect of this royal parade on:
a) Haman?

b) Mordecai?

c) The Jewish population?

d) The Persian population?

DAY 4 *Esther 6:14–7:2 (Contrast Song of Solomon [Song of Songs NIV] 2:4).*
a) How would you describe the atmosphere in the banquet room?

b) Comment on the state of mind of each of the three participants.

c) How can we affect the atmosphere of our homes, church meetings, work places, etc.?

DAY 5 *Esther 7:3, 4; 4:14; Psalm 62:1; Isaiah 30:18.*
a) Esther knows that the time of her request has come. What benefit had come from the delay of one day?

b) For whom does she ask mercy?

c) She could have endured slavery. That has happened many times to the Jews before and since. But she knows God cannot allow total annihilation. Why? (Gen. 49:10; Jer. 16:14, 15; Zech. 8:8; etc.).

DAY 6 *Esther 7:5-8.*
a) Contrast Esther's courage and directness with her former fear (*4:11-16*). What had brought about the change ?

b) How can difficulties bring about a greater maturity in us?

DAY 7 *Esther 7:9, 10; Psalm 37:35-37; Proverbs 26:27; James 2:13.*
a) The jigsaw of Haman's plot is now fitting into place in the king's mind as he hears about the gallows erected for Mordecai. What may the king have learned from this whole episode?

b) For the Christian, even the difficulties in our lives and our failures, may be redemptive. True of false?

NOTES

HAMAN'S PRIDE ...

Haman's pride comes to fruition in this section, and finally it brings about his destruction.

In this he is a picture of Satan who fell from his eminence through pride (Isa. 14:12–15; Ezek. 28:11–19). Let us look at some of the evidence of Haman's pride that we see in these chapters:

1. His pride is mortally hurt when Mordecai still refuses to tremble before him, even after knowing of the death sentence on his nation,

2. His pride causes him to boast of his position and wealth to his family and friends.

3. Through his pride he eagerly agrees with his wife's evil counsel to get Mordecai publicly hanged. He couldn't endure a further nine months of Mordecai not cowering before him.

4. His pride assures him that he alone must be the man whom the king delights to honour.

... AND ITS RESULTS

1. Loss of friends: servants, his family and finally the king became disillusioned with his conceit.

2. Humiliation: Jesus said, 'Everyone who exalts himself shall be humbled' (Luke 18:14).

Imagine the mortification Haman went through as he acted as servant to Mordecai, and conducted him in royal attire through the city! Imagine the mocking he received as he called out 'This is the man whom the king delights to honour!' It was only his conceit that had brought him into this place of humiliation.

3. Destruction: Public execution by hanging (the death he had planned for Mordecai), was to be the fate of a man whose whole life had been motivated by pride and conceit.

LESSONS FOR US

Haman's pride probably started in a small way but, as he fed it, it grew till it became the consuming passion of his life and brought him to destruction. We all have this tendency in varying degrees and appearing in different guises. The opposite to feeding it is to starve it. As we look to Jesus who, though the Son of God, was yet so gentle and lowly in heart, and look to the price He paid to free us from our sin and pride, we can only bow in humility and love before Him. There is a needy world all around us. Let us take our eyes off ourselves, and ask Him to make us channels of His love to those we contact.

MEMORY VERSE: Take my yoke upon you and learn from me, for I am gentle and humble in heart, and you will find rest for your souls' (Matt. 11:29, NIV).

STUDY 9

DELIVERANCE FOR THE NATION

QUESTIONS

DAY 1   *Esther 8:1, 2; Job 5:11; John 3:20, 21; 1 Corinthians 15:24.*
a) The king promoted Mordecai from the rank of a minor officer to the rank of Prime Minister in Haman's place. What immediate effect would that have among the Jews of the city?

b) Esther is not looking for honours for herself but for Mordecai. Is there a spiritual message for ourselves in this?

DAY 2   *Esther 8:3-8; Romans 9:1-3; 10:1.*
a) Esther knows that she and her cousin would now be protected. But for whom is she concerned?

b) If we belong to Christ, how should our concern for others be shown?

DAY 3   *Esther 8:9-14; Mark 1:22; Luke 9:1; John 5:27-30; 7:16-18; 2 Corinthians 10:8; Ephesians 1:19-23.*
a) King Ahasuerus gave to Mordecai the ring of authority to defeat Haman's evil plans and to save the Jews. This is a picture of the authority God gave to Jesus. For what purpose?

b) To whom has Jesus now given this authority?

DAY 4   *Esther 8:15-17; Matthew 25:23; Hebrews 11:1, 6; Romans 4:20, 21; 12:12a.*
a) Mordecai now receives the honour Haman had coveted for himself (6:7, 8). With this in mind comment on Luke 14:11.

b) How are verses 16 and 17 a lesson for us in faith?

DAY 5   *Esther 9:1-5; Hebrews 2:14, 15.*
a) Haman obviously had a strong, well-organized movement afoot to destroy the Jews. What had contributed to their loss of morale?

b) At what do Satan's hosts tremble? (*Ps. 133; Zech. 4:6, 7; Luke 9:1; 10:17-19; Eph. 6:10-18; James 2:19.*)

DAY 6   *Esther 9:6-10; Proverbs 16:29; 28:10; Hebrews 12:15.*
Why were the ten sons of Haman destroyed? (Note: They were all named.)

DAY 7   *Esther 9:11-16; Ephesians 6:12; Revelation 12:9-11.*
a) It sounds as if Esther shows a very bloodthirsty trait here, but if we knew the whole story we would understand. Why do you think she asked for a further day of vengeance? And for the hanging of Haman's sons?

b) What shows us that the Jews, as God's people, had no mercenary motives, but slew only those who were a threat to their existence as a race?

c) This incident took place before Jesus taught us the new way of 'grace' (John 1:17). If we were threatened in a similar way today, what would be our attitude? (Matt. 5:43, 44; 1 Pet. 2:20-23; 4:12-16.)

NOTES

Although Haman was dead, his evil works continued after him. Esther and Mordecai were safe, but the edicts condemning their brothers to destruction were still on display in every town in the vast empire. Mordecai and Esther could not be complacent about the destruction of their people.

Spiritually, what message do we see in this? Judicially, Satan, our enemy, has been condemned through Christ's death on the cross, and his doom is sealed. But his evil works are still on display everywhere and all the more as he knows his time is now short (Rev. 12:12). In view of this, what can we learn from the attitude of Mordecai and Esther?

1. *Concern*: Esther wept.
2. *Intercession*: She pleaded with the king, and he authorized her to act.
3. *Service*: With the king's permission, Mordecai and Esther conscripted an army of scribes to write copies of decrees in every language, authorizing the Jews to gather together to fight their enemies. An army of mounted horsemen carried the message to the whole empire, regardless of expense involved. Many human lives were at stake.

Can you see a pattern here for getting the message of deliverance out to all the world?

The first need is CONCERN, then INTERCESSION, then practical SERVICE. This includes going, sending out messengers, publishing and distributing the liberating Word of God, and financial support. The matter is urgent.

PREPARATION FOR DELIVERANCE
Though the former decree, sealed with the king's seal, could not be annulled, the latter decree carried much more weight. It gave the Jews exactly the same authority that had previously been given to their enemies. They were to 'kill, slay and annihilate' all those in this anti-Semitic movement that Haman had organized. To this end they were to gather together and present a united front against a common foe. The news would spread quickly that the king was on the side of the Jews, and that his queen and prime minister were of the Jewish race. Also that Haman, their leader, was dead. No wonder that fear fell on all the thousands of enemies who had planned their destruction and the looting of their property. Even before the victory was won, the people of God grew in confidence and assurance.

THE DELIVERANCE
The 13th day of the 12th month arrived, and what happened? Not only were God's people protected so that not one was killed, but thousands of their enemies perished. So Haman's 'lucky day', determined by casting lots, proved again that God is in control, not chance (Prov. 16:33).

Mordecai now became much more powerful than Haman had ever been. God wants us to recognize the greatness and power of our 'Mordecai', and to work together with Him towards the day when we shall see the final destruction of all Satan's forces. That day is surely coming.

MEMORY VERSE: 'All authority in heaven and on earth has been given to me. Therefore go and make disciples of all nations' (Matt. 28:18, 19, NIV).

ESTHER • STUDY 9 • DELIVERANCE FOR THE NATION • • • • • • •

33

STUDY 10

FEAST OF PURIM

QUESTIONS

DAY 1   *Esther 9:17-19, 23; 2 Chronicles 20:27-29; Ezra 6:22; Nehemiah 12:27.*
a) How did the Jews celebrate their victory?

b) What are some reasons we, as Christians, have for rejoicing? (Luke 10:20; John 4:36; Phil. 4:4; 1 Pet. 1:3-6; 2 John 4.)

DAY 2   *Esther 9:20-22; 2 Chronicles 7:14; Isaiah 52:1, 2; 61:3; John 17:21.*
a) What were some of the means God had used to turn the nation 'from sorrow into gladness, and mourning into a holiday'?

b) What were the greatest benefits that had come to the Jews from the traumatic experiences of the past year?

DAY 3   *Esther 9:23-26; Psalm 25:4, 9; Romans 12:1, 2.*
a) The word 'Purim' was from Pur meaning 'lot', as Haman had found his auspicious day by casting lots. What does the result of his 'lucky day' teach us about superstitions?

b) God did tolerate casting lots before Pentecost (Acts 1:23-26). Can a Christian rely on this means to find out God's will ('heads I go, tails I stay')? What is a better way to seek God's guidance?

DAY 4   *Esther 9:27, 28; Genesis 18:19; Deuteronomy 4:9, 40; 11:19; 30:2, 3; 32:46; 1 Kings 2:4.*
a) Why was Mordecai so sure that the celebration of Purim would not die out after a few years?

b) What can Christian parents learn from this?

DAY 5   *Esther 9:29-32; Mark 16:20; 1 Corinthians 3:9; 2 Corinthians 5:20; Hebrews 2:3, 4; Titus 2:1-8.*
a) 'Mordecai the Jew' has ceased to be a title of derision and has now become a title of honour (as 'Haman the Agagite', v. 24, is now a title of dishonour). Discuss whether people judge our nation, our family, our church, etc., by our character and conduct.

b) We now see Mordecai and Esther in real partnership (Queen Esther has now come into a place of authority, v. 32). What does this teach us about the relationship of Christ and the church?

DAY 6   *Esther 10:2; 2 Chronicles 19:9; Nehemiah 2:10; Daniel 6:4; Matthew 25:40; Luke 16:10.*
a) Why did King Ahasuerus raise Mordecai the gatekeeper to a position next to himself, so that he found a place, not only in Israel's but in Persian history books?

b) Why was he so beloved by his own Jewish people?

DAY 7   Share with the group the aspects on the studies on 'Esther' that have blessed you most.

One of the most joyous feasts of the Jews, which is still celebrated 2,400 years after the Book of ESTHER was written, is the Feast of Purim. It is celebrated on the 14th day of the 12th month, which corresponds roughly to our month of March. It marks the triumph of the Jewish people over their enemies, and is marked by much joy, feasting and exchanging of gifts. During their synagogue service the entire Book of ESTHER is read aloud, with acclamation at every mention of Mordecai and booing for Haman!

The incidents of ESTHER are not unique in Jewish history. Perhaps they are the most persecuted people on earth throughout their 4,000 years of turbulent history. From AD 70 till this generation, they have been scattered throughout the earth, but now many have returned to their inheritance. We owe much to Israel. They were God's chosen nation, through whom God gave to the world the Old Testament scriptures and the Saviour, our Lord Jesus Christ. We look forward to Israel's return, not only to their land, but in repentance and faith to the Saviour they rejected. In the meantime, we rejoice with them in their celebration of Purim, their Feast of Deliverance.

OUR CELEBRATION OF DELIVERANCE

If the Jewish people have so much to rejoice about in their Feast of Deliverance we have more! We, too, are a chosen race. Peter said about us, the Church of Jesus Christ: 'But you are a chosen people, a royal priesthood, a holy nation, a people belonging to God, that you may declare the praises of him who called you out of darkness into his wonderful light' (I Pet. 2:9, NIV).

Like the Jewish people we too have our special celebrations – Christmas, Easter, the Holy Communion, etc., and yet it is so easy for us to take part in all these reminders of the victory Jesus has bought for us, and still not experience true deliverance.

Jesus died on the cross, not only to save us from the punishment our sins deserve, but to free us to live joyous, victorious lives. Has He delivered YOU from sin, guilt, fear and depression? Jesus wants to do that for each one of us, and He WILL do it if we sincerely desire it. Then we do not need to rely on any special days to remind us of His deliverance, for the Deliverer Himself comes to live within us!

OUR DECLARATION OF DELIVERANCE

In the verse quoted above, Peter reminds us of our job here on earth: 'That you may declare the wonderful deeds of Him Who called you out of darkness into His marvellous light.' First we must know in experience that Jesus has rescued us from Satan's darkness, and brought us into God's own family. If this is your experience then He calls YOU to share that good news. Esther and Mordecai were very ordinary people and He chose and used them. Most of us are pretty ordinary people too. Read I Corinthians 1:27-29. Are you in this category? Then you qualify to be a bearer of the good news of a Saviour and Deliverer to others.

MEMORY VERSE: I Peter 2:9 (quoted above).

ANSWER GUIDE

The following pages contain an Answer Guide. It is recommended that answers to the questions be attempted before turning to this guide. It is only a guide and the answers given should not be treated as exhaustive.

GUIDE TO INTRODUCTORY STUDY

Select two members of your group who could take the roles of Ruth and Esther, and read their portions clearly and confidently. Make sure they have the material beforehand, so they can become familiar with the text.

If you feel the group would be sufficiently confident to discuss together any points arising from the playette, with your guidance, by all means do so.

Encourage the group to put time and thought into preparation for each week's study, and to come with written answers to the set questions. They will get more from the preparation of their answers if they prepare the allotted portion each day, rather than at one or two sittings.

The Memory Verses for each week have been written in full in the New International Version, so that the class will be memorizing the verses in the same wording. It will be good if they attempt to memorize these portions in advance, and some time be given in class to revise and repeat the verses together. Though the Memory Verses are given in the NIV, members should be encouraged to use and/or refer to as many other translations as possible in the preparations of the studies.

* * *

There should be some thought provoking discussion as the group goes through the references on 'Grace and Grit'. It would be good to close the Introductory Study with a time of prayer asking that each member will be encouraged to go forward into the ten weeks' study expectant of growth in grace and confident trust in the Lord.

GUIDE TO STUDY 1

DAY I a) They moved to Moab because of the famine in Judah. Seeking comfort and advice from non-Christians rather than from the people of God, and looking for a way of escape from a difficult situation.

b) In submission to God in prayer, repentance and seeking His leading. By remaining in the love and encouragement of His people.

DAY 2 Mixed marriage between people of two races is not unscriptural, so long as both parties are believers; marriage between non-Christian and Christian is against the teaching of the Bible. The main ingredient for a successful marriage is lacking, and frequently leads to compromise on the part of the Christian.

DAY 3 a) The knowledge that food was now available, also the realization that tragedy had come to her while away from God and His people.
b) Some non-Christians have had a more secure and loving upbringing than some Christians. Nevertheless, the Christian who still has problems arising from his past has the power to overcome them, and is a 'nicer' person than he would have been without the Lord.

DAY 4 a) Security, hope of a second marriage, preference for her ancestral gods.
b) Jesus insisted that people first count the cost.
c) Those who don't can either make a false commitment or become easily defeated and discouraged when problems and trials come their way.

DAY 5 a) Love and sympathy for Naomi. Faith in Naomi's God.
b) Fear of the unknown; fear of being despised as a foreigner; poverty; insecurity (especially if Naomi should die); unlikelihood of marriage.

DAY 6 a) We can expect loving forgiveness from God and His people should we go through a time of backsliding. Likewise, we must always be eager to welcome 'home' anyone who has strayed away from God and His people.
b) They hardly expected to see her again after an absence of ten years. They would be shocked to see her bereft of husband and sons, with the consequent marks of suffering on her face. She would look much older and more frail.

DAY 7 a) She blamed God for her misfortunes and doubted His love. Was full of self-pity, and even bitterness at the trials which had come her way.
b) To admit she had been wrong and God had disciplined her, but to look forward with hope to the future.

GUIDE TO STUDY 2

DAY 1 Boaz was a wealthy man of standing in the community, whereas Ruth was a penniless stranger. Boaz also seems to be a much older person.

DAY 2 a) Israel was not a 'Welfare State', and this was God's appointed provision for the poor.
On the whole, yes.
b) Submission and respect from Ruth; wise and loving leadership from Naomi.

DAY 3   a) Saul 'happening' to reach Samuel's village in search of his donkeys at the time God wanted him anointed to be king.
Rebecca 'happening' to come to draw water at the time the servant was praying God to show His choice.
The Samaritan woman 'happening' to come to draw water while Jesus was resting at the well, etc.
b) We can receive God's guidance naturally while going about our usual duties. God delights to guide His children, often through circumstances, and there is nothing mystical or complicated about it, so long as we desire to do God's will.

DAY 4   a) Mutual respect and consideration, especially in a firm which is founded on Christian principles.
b) Husband and wife, parents and children, church officers and members, teacher and class, shop assistant and customer, etc.
c) To desire another's happiness and welfare. The Lord, our Christian brothers and sisters, our enemies, everyone.

DAY 5   a) (I) Boaz: Thankfulness, respect, thoughtfulness, encouragement, reverence, right use of authority, etc.
(2) Ruth: Humility but not servility, industriousness, appreciation, thankfulness, joy, etc.
b) Yes, by instructing the reapers to drop grain on purpose for her. By doing more than is expected of us.

DAY 6   a) Probably a battle between faith and anxiety.
b) An ephah of barley—more than she could possibly have gleaned. Roasted barley (popcorn!) she had saved from her lunch for Naomi.

DAY 7   By showing them love, caring, encouragement. By showing them that God has a solution to their problems.

GUIDE TO STUDY 3

DAY I   The Lord as our shepherd, shelter, rock, deliverer, fortress, shield, stronghold. The Name of the Lord as our strong tower. The blood of Christ. The spiritual armour God has provided.

DAY 2   To meet our spiritual bridegroom we need:
I. WASHING of rebirth, the Word of God, baptism.
2. ANOINTING with the power of the Holy Spirit.
3. GARMENTS of righteousness, salvation, praise.

DAY 3   a) To God, to husbands, to employers, to elders of the church, to rulers, to one another.
b) Jesus Christ.

DAY 4   a) By being unwilling to entertain relatives, help shoulder their burdens, etc. By neglecting to care for aged parents.
b) Enquiry regarding their needs, letters, phone calls, invitations, offers to mind children, elderly, etc.

DAY 5   a) The Gentile woman is now a believer
b) Deborah, Esther, Abigail, Hannah, Mary (mother of Jesus), Elizabeth, Mary and Martha, Mary Magdalene, Dorcas, Phoebe, Priscilla.

DAY 6   a) His integrity. Also his faith that God, not man, was in control.
b) By concealing the fact that she had been there, in case people misinterpreted the purpose of her visit.

DAY 7   a) Feelings probably ranging from anxiety to hope, doubt to full assurance of faith.
b) He was a man with firmness of purpose. When he knew what was the right thing to do he got on with it; didn't procrastinate.

GUIDE TO STUDY 4

DAY 1   a) Whether the nearer kinsman was prepared to redeem Elimelech's property and marry Ruth.
b) Yes.

DAY 2   a) Because the sons of his first marriage could not inherit Elimelech's property, but the son (hopefully) to be born to Ruth. This could cause tensions between the two wives and their children. Also, he might have another large family to provide for.
b) Relief and praise to God.

DAY 3   a) The rejected widow was to spit in his face, as well as removing his sandal.
b) Voluntary. Jesus voluntarily became man and bore our sins on the cross to redeem us to God.

DAY 4   a) The list found in Galatians 5:22, 23. Also our witness, whereby we win people to Christ.
b) Jesus Christ, who was Boaz's and Ruth's descendent was born in Bethlehem.

DAY 5   a) The husband is to love his wife as Christ loved the Church, and the wife is to respect and love her husband.
b) Love on Christ's part, and loving obedience on ours. On Christ's return.

DAY 6   a) Willingness to let the grandparents have a share in caring for the child, and willingness on grandparents' part to help in this way.
b) Sensitivity required from both sides. Mother-in-law and daughter-in-law can get along well together, if the relationship is worked at.

DAY 7   a) Joseph's brothers' unkindness to him was overruled by God to preserve their lives.
Peter's denial of Jesus cured him of his self-assurance and changed him to a humble, dependent man.
In these and other cases, repentance was required before God's grace overruled their mistakes.
b) No. It more often leads to compromise of Christian standards on the part of the believer.
Personal.

GUIDE TO STUDY 5

DAY 1   The Persian kingdom was very great and wealthy. King Ahasuerus, like Nebuchadnezzar and Belshazzar, was proud, extravagant, looking for admiration and popularity from his subjects.

DAY 2   a) He was proud of her beauty and wanted further to impress his guests.
b) It is debatable whether she did right or wrong. She, no doubt, shrank from being a 'show-piece', yet was letting down her husband's authority as king; perhaps the fact that he was drunk affected her decision. Submission as far as conscience allows. On most issues agreement can be reached by talking the matter over.

DAY 3   a) That Queen Vashti should be replaced by one better than she.
b) Probably. It would soon get around that the queen had disobeyed her husband, and other wives would tend to copy her example.

DAY 4   a) Must be a virgin. Chosen on physical beauty and charm alone.
b) Love. Commitment to each other for life. Mutual trust and caring for the partner. Sharing. Interest in each other's concerns. Readiness to apologise and forgive. Praying together. Christ at the centre. (You may have other suggestions.)

DAY 5   a) He was a Jew of the tribe of Benjamin. He was compassionate, and adopted his young cousin, treating her just as a daughter.

b) Beauty is of face and figure. Lovely indicates a loving personality that attracts others. Even if not beautiful, we can cultivate that inner beauty which is often more attractive than mere physical beauty.

Great concern, though Mordecai would probably be pleased that his 'daughter' was considered such a beauty!

They would both probably be in prayer about the outcome and take it as God's will.

DAY 6   God has allowed me to be in this situation. He is with me and will bring about His purposes, and will give needed grace. (See Gen. 50:20 and Rom. 8:28.)

DAY 7   a) Probably a mixture of pleasure and nervousness, with an assurance that God is in control.

b) Disappointment. Women in most countries today know a freedom never known in history.

GUIDE TO STUDY 6

DAY 1   a) Daniel and his three friends. Nehemiah.

b) By keeping aware of current events, praying for those in authority. By using our influence for good, such as getting on school committees, writing letters to local MP, newspaper where indicated. By keeping our country's laws, paying due taxes. By avoiding negative criticism of our government.

DAY 2   a) In the home, schools, church, politics, industry, etc.

b) In our looks, dress, attainments, spiritual progress and abilities, in material possessions.

Remember God is the Giver and Enabler. Keep laying down the temptation at the Cross, and trust Christ for victory.

DAY 3   a) Joseph, Jeremiah, Gideon, Daniel and three friends, etc.

b) Abraham and Isaac in saying their wife was a sister. Pilate, Judas, Peter, etc.

DAY 4   a) Hitler who during the Second World War tried to annihilate the Jews.

b) By temptation to sin, doubt, fear, depression, lethargy, etc. Also, by seeking to hinder the spread of the gospel, attacking by illness, accidents, and direct persecution of Christians.

c) Pray with compassion, give, write encouraging letters, etc.

DAY 5	a) Because of blind trust in him and a desire to please his favourite. Greed.
	b) To think things out carefully instead of making rash decisions.
DAY 6	To resist the devil and undo his evil works.
	The Word of God, the blood of Christ, the power and anointing of the Holy Spirit, the name of Jesus, the whole armour of God.
DAY 7	Personal testimony. Going. Giving. Publication and distribution of God's Word and tracts. Keeping ourselves informed. Praying intelligently with faith. The media.

GUIDE TO STUDY 7

DAY 1	a) Mourning, weeping, fasting, wailing, wearing sackcloth and ashes.
	b) '3', unless you have something preferable for '4'.
DAY 2	a) Seek to be informed in every way possible. Mix with other types of people besides Christians. Ask God to show us needs to pray about and help where possible.
	b) Sin can't be hidden. It has a way of getting out.
DAY 3	a) To go to the king to plead with him for her people.
	b) 1. Our families; 2. Our church fellowship; 3. Our nation; 4. The human race.
DAY 4	a) Your own words.
	b) Acceptance and contentment in our lot, and an active seeking of the ministry God has for us in it.
DAY 5	a) Daniel in finding out the meaning of the dream.
	The Church gathering to pray for Peter in prison; for the sending out of the apostles Paul and Barnabas, etc. The support and concern of the group strengthens faith and releases God's power.
	b) It helps to put to death our fleshly desires, to concentrate on seeking God, enables us to have extra time to do so. It releases power for the spiritual warfare against Satan. It is beneficial to the health. (See I Cor. 7:5; Matt. 4:2; 17:21; etc.)
DAY 6	Garments of praise, salvation and righteousness. (See the rendering of Isa. 61:3 in the Good News Bible).

DAY 7 She felt in her spirit that God had not yet prepared the way. She would naturally be nervous and would be waiting on God for the right opportunity which had not yet come.

GUIDE TO STUDY 8

DAY 1 a) By embittering our spirit, and taking our minds off Christ, the source of joy. It causes pain to the one hated and to his/her loved ones.
b) It can cause others to take sides and cause disruption.

DAY 2 a) The king unable to sleep that particular night; the timing of Rebecca coming to the well; Samuel meeting Saul; Jesus being born. Of all the scrolls of the chronicles that could have been read, he read the part about Mordecai's good deed. Haman's arrival at the moment the king wanted some suggestion of a fitting reward. The incident happened on the day Esther had planned to expose Haman's treachery.
b) Personal.

DAY 3 a) Haman: Mortification.
b) Mordecai: Surprise and reassurance that God is working things out.
c) The Jewish population: Jubilation.
d) The Persian population: Bewilderment.

DAY 4 a) Tense.
b) Haman: Apprehensive.
The king: Curious, puzzled.
Queen Esther: Nervous, but gaining assurance.
c) Negatively: by anger, worry, self-centredness, lethargy.
Positively: by showing joy, enthusiasm, encouragement, love.
The former attitude deadens the atmosphere; the latter lifts it.

DAY 5 a) God had worked in the meantime to prepare the king to hear Esther's complaint against Haman. The king had been reminded of Mordecai's loyalty and had probably sensed Haman's hatred of him.
b) For herself and her people.
c) 1. Because God had promised they would return from captivity.
2. She knew God must be faithful to the nation He had chosen.
3. The promised Messiah was to be born from the tribe of Judah.

DAY 6 a) A new sense of responsibility for her people, and the assurance that she, in her position as queen, was the one God had chosen to bring deliverance. Prayer and fasting had contributed to the change in her attitude.
b) Difficulties bring about a greater dependence on God, as well as a deeper sympathy with others in trouble.

DAY 7   a) Not to be so gullible, but learn the facts thoroughly before making decisions.
b) True, so long as we are humble enough to learn from them.

GUIDE TO STUDY 9

DAY 1   a) Joy, and hope for deliverance.
b) In any service we do for God and for His people, we should desire Jesus' Name to be exalted, not our own.

DAY 2   a) For the whole nation of the Jews who are still in danger.
b) By sympathy, practical service and prayer.

DAY 3   a) To represent the Father in His character, teaching and works of deliverance from the power of Satan, and finally to judge the world.
b) To His body, the Church.

DAY 4   a) Mordecai had humbled himself in mourning, prayer and fasting. Now God has exalted him to a place of authority and power.
b) The Jews rejoiced in anticipation of victory before actually seeing the victory.

DAY 5   a) Their leader, Haman, was dead, and the king had exalted the leader of the despised Jews to Haman's position. The nationality of Queen Esther would also have leaked out.
b) Satan trembles where God's people are unitedly displaying the love, power and authority of Christ.

DAY 6   Because they were probably well known as leaders in this movement against the Jews. The whole family, including his wife, were contaminated by Haman's hatred of the Jews.

DAY 7   a) Because she probably knew that there were others in the plot against the Jews who, if not destroyed, could later be a source of danger. Perhaps it was known that some of Haman's friends had gone into hiding.
b) They refused to take the loot of their destroyed enemies, even though authorized to do so.
c) To seek to break down opposition by love, prayer and trust in God. To endure suffering patiently, as many of our brethren in less favoured lands are doing today, knowing that after the suffering comes the glory.

GUIDE TO STUDY 10

DAY 1   a) By joy, feasting, giving presents to each other and to the poor, by singing and music.

b) Our names are written in heaven. We have a living hope of an inheritance in heaven. We know Jesus as our Saviour and Lord.
Joy in winning people to Christ and in seeing Christians progressing in the faith.

DAY 2   a) Through bringing about national repentance, resulting in the defeat of their enemy, Haman, and the raising up of Mordecai and Esther as their deliverers, also in turning the king's heart towards the Jewish nation.
b) A return to God in repentance and faith, and a renewing in them of a sense of their national identity as God's people.

DAY 3   a) That they are nonsense.
b) God may on occasion guide an uninstructed Christian in this way, but it is not God's ideal method.
First we must desire God's will, not our own. Pray about it, and God often guides by an inner knowing, confirming this by His Word, by circumstances, and by discussion with trusted spiritual leaders.

DAY 4   a) Because it was Jewish custom to teach their children to respect and obey their parents and their spiritual leaders.
b) That it is the duty of Christian parents to teach their children the Word of God, by precept as well as by example. Sunday School can reinforce, but not take the place of parental teaching.

DAY 5   a) They take notice of what we are rather than what we say.
b) That we are to work in partnership. Christ now works through His church.

DAY 6   a) He had been proved faithful in small things, so the king knew he could trust him to fill a position of importance.
b) Because he cared about them, and spared no effort to save and serve them.

DAY 7   Personal application.

GEARED FOR GROWTH BIBLE STUDIES

Enable you to:

1. Have a daily encounter with God
2. Encourage you to apply the Word of God to everyday life
3. Help you to share your faith with others
4. They are straightforward, practical, non-controversial and inexpensive.

WEC INTERNATIONAL is involved in gospel outreach, church planting and discipleship training using every possible means including radio, literature, medical work, rural development schemes, correspondence courses and telephone counselling. Nearly two thousand workers are involved in their fields and sending bases.

Find out more from the following Website:
www.wec-int.org.uk

A full list of over 50 'Geared for Growth' studies can be obtained from:

UK GEARED FOR GROWTH COORDINATORS
John and Ann Edwards
8, Sidings Terrace, Skewen, Neath, W.Glam, SA10 6RE
Email: rhysjohn.edwards@virgin.net
Tel. 01792 814994

UK Website: www.gearedforgrowth.co.uk

For information on Geared for Growth Bible Studies in other languages contact:

Word Worldwide International Coordinators
Kip and Doreen Wear
Tel. 01269 870842
Email: kip.wear@virgin.net

RUTH & ESTHER • ANSWER GUIDE • • • • • •

Christian Focus Publications
Publishes books for all ages

Our mission statement –
STAYING FAITHFUL
In dependence upon God we seek to help make His infallible word, the Bible, relevant.
Our aim is to ensure that the Lord Jesus Christ is presented as the only hope to obtain
forgiveness of sin, live a useful life and look forward to heaven with Him.
REACHING OUT
Christ's last command requires us to reach out to our world with His gospel. We seek to
help fulfil that by publishing books that point people towards Jesus and help them to
develop a Christ-like maturity. We aim to equip all levels of readers for life, work, ministry
and mission.

Books in our adult range are published in three imprints.
Christian Focus contains popular works including biographies, commentaries, basic
doctrine, and Christian living. Our children's books are published in this imprint.
Mentor focuses on books written at a level suitable for Bible College and seminary
students, pastors, and other serious readers. The imprint includes commentaries,
doctrinal studies, examination of current issues, and church history.
Christian Heritage contains classic writings from the past.

For details of our titles visit us on our website
www.christianfocus.com

ISBN 978-1-85792-908-9
Copyright © WEC International
Published in 2003,
Reprinted 2008
by
Christian Focus Publications,
Geanies House, Fearn, Ross-shire,
IV20 ITW, Scotland
and
WEC International,
Bulstrode, Oxford Road, Gerrards Cross, Bucks, SL9 8SZ

Cover design by Alister MacInnes
Printed and bound by Bell & Bain Ltd., Glasgow